THE FACTS ABOUT
Arthritis

Claire Llewellyn

Belitha Press

First published in the UK in 2001 by
Belitha Press Limited
London House, Great Eastern Wharf
Parkgate Road, London SW11 4NQ

Copyright © Belitha Press Limited 2001
Text by Claire Llewellyn
Illustration by Tom Connell

Editor: Russell McLean
Designer: Helen James
Picture researcher: Frances Vargo
Clinical consultant: Frankie Turner, Senior Occupational
    Therapist, Yorkshire Regional Juvenile Arthritis Service

Quotes on pages 10 and 21 are taken from Arthritis Today magazine.

Splint shown on page 15 supplied by Wristeasy, PO Box 135,
Wetherby, West Yorkshire, LS23 7JJ

ISBN 1 84138 312 0

Printed in China

10 9 8 7 6 5 4 3 2 1

British Library Cataloguing in Publication Data
for this book is available from the British Library.

Picture acknowledgements:
John Birdsall Photography: 5t, 23b. Corbis: Chris Carroll 12; Jenny Woodcock/
Reflections Photolibrary 26b, 27. Eye Ubiquitous: James Davis Travel
Photography 29; Yiorgos Nikiteas 4t; Paul Seheult 20, 21t; Skjold 10. Sally
& Richard Greenhill: Sally Greenhill 3l, 5b, 22b. Photofusion: Richard Alton
28b; Paul Baldesare cover background, 4b, 13b; Richard Galloway 9b; Crispin
Hughes 24t; Clarissa Leahy 8b; Brian Mitchell 1, 24b. Rex Features: Vic
Thomasson 22t. Robert Harding Picture Library: 8t, 25t; E. Chino 3r, 19t.
Science Photo Library: Bill Bachmann 7b; John Banosi cover br, 6t; CC Studio
cover bc, 16b; BSIP Edwige 17t; BSIP Leca 18b, 21b; BSIP Taulin 17b; Alain
Dix/Publiphoto Diffusion 7t; John Greim 14b, 18t; Richard Hutchings 26t;
Dr. P. Marazzi 15b. Stock Market: Jose Luis Pelaez Inc. 11b; Ariel Skelly 16t;
Tom Stewart 28t. Telegraph Colour Library: Candice Farmer cover bl, 3c, 25b;
Chris Ladd 14t; Barbara Peacock 9t; Martin Riedl 19b; Geoff Tompkinson 13t.
David Towersey: 11t, 15t, 23t.

Contents

Words in **bold** are explained
in the glossary on page 30

What is arthritis?

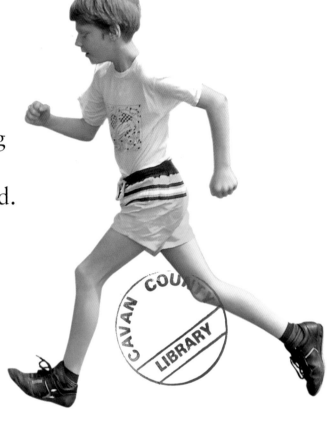

Arthritis is a disease which affects the body's **joints**. It makes them feel stiff and painful. We use our joints every time we move, so having arthritis not only hurts, but makes it difficult to get around.

Children with arthritis

Most of us think that only older people have arthritis. This is not true. Many children and young people have a form of arthritis known as **juvenile chronic arthritis**.

We can bend, twist and straighten our bodies because our bones fit together at places called joints.

Clues to arthritis

You can't always tell that someone has arthritis, but now and again there are obvious signs. These signs are known as **symptoms**.

Children who have arthritis don't let it stop them having fun.

Arthritis symptoms

- Pain and swelling in the joints.
- Feeling very stiff.
- Difficulty in moving.
- Feeling tired and generally unwell.

This is how some people with arthritis describe their symptoms:

'My knee hurts when I have to stand.'

'I feel really stiff when I get up in the morning and when it gets cold.'

'I can't move as fast as other people.'

'I get tired very quickly.'

'I can't keep up with my friends.'

Most people think that only older people have arthritis. This is not true – many young people have it, too.

Living with arthritis

Arthritis can be painful. Some people have mild arthritis, which means there may be times when they cannot run. Others have severe arthritis, which means they are unable to run at all. One of the difficult things about arthritis in young people is that it varies a lot from day to day; and it may last for a few months or for many years. Doctors can't tell what the future holds.

There is often no way of telling from the outside whether someone has juvenile arthritis.

Looking at joints

Joints are places where two bones meet. They have to take a lot of wear and tear. If joints are affected by arthritis, they become painful and may be permanently damaged.

Moving easily

In a joint, smooth **cartilage** covers the ends of the bones. It stops the bones from grinding together and wearing away. An oily liquid called **synovial fluid** coats the joint. This helps it to move smoothly and easily, over and over again.

The joints shown in red are the ones most often affected by arthritis.

Inflamed joints

Joints that are affected by arthritis become **inflamed**. In other words, they are red, tender and warm to the touch.

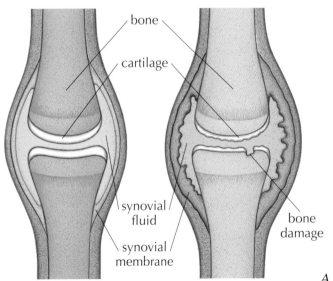

bone

cartilage

synovial fluid

synovial membrane

bone damage

A normal joint

A joint affected by arthritis

A knee joint that is affected by arthritis becomes swollen and painful.

Arthritis can also cause:

- Inflammation in the eyes, which may lead to serious eye disease.
- **Anaemia** (a lack of red blood cells).
- Tiredness and irritability.
- Loss of appetite and weight.

An inflamed joint, such as this elbow joint, is red, swollen and stiff.

Thinning cartilage

An inflamed joint makes too much synovial fluid. This builds up around the joint – making it swollen and causing pain and stiffness when the joint is moved. Over a long time, the inflammation can make the layers of cartilage at the ends of the bones grow thinner. Without treatment, this may cause damage to the bones.

Did you know?

- Arthritis comes from the Greek word *arthron*, meaning joint. *Itis* means inflammation.
- Arthritis is a physical condition. It affects the body, not the mind, but it can affect the way you feel.

Preventing damage

Bones are living **tissue** and can heal themselves as they grow. But a joint that has been damaged by inflammation may not be able to do this. Treatment for arthritis aims to calm the inflammation. This makes a person's joints feel less painful and stiff today, and may prevent damage in the future.

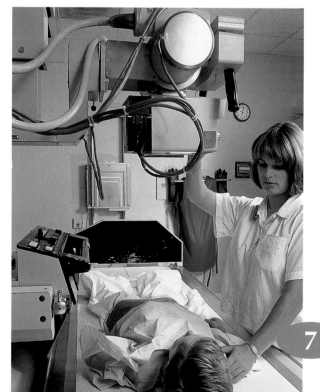

X-rays *help doctors to look inside the body and see the condition of a person's joints.*

Types of arthritis

Arthritis is a general name that covers a large number of conditions affecting the joints.

Childhood arthritis
Three types of arthritis affect young people in particular – **oligo-articular**, **poly-articular** and **systemic onset arthritis**. All three are grouped under the general name of juvenile chronic arthritis.

Oligo-articular arthritis
This affects about two-thirds of all children with arthritis. Less than five joints are swollen, and sometimes only the knee. The condition can make children feel ill, but often improves after a few years.

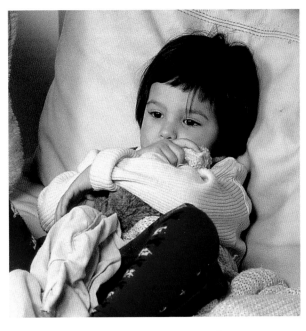

Oligo-articular arthritis can make a child feel generally unwell.

Poly-articular arthritis
This affects one in five children with arthritis. Five or more joints are inflamed, making a child very tired and unwilling to move. It often comes on quickly, and spreads from one joint to another. Some children recover within a year, but many have the condition for longer. The longer the arthritis lasts, the more likely there is to be damage to the joints.

Poly-articular arthritis is tiring, as it affects many of the body's joints.

8

Systemic onset arthritis

This affects one in ten children with arthritis. Most are under five years old. It starts with a high temperature and a red, blotchy rash on the arms and legs. At first, these symptoms can be mistaken for an infection. It may be weeks before there is any pain in the joints. Systemic onset arthritis leaves a child pale, weak and **vulnerable** to infections.

Systemic onset arthritis starts with a high temperature. It can last for several years.

Ups and downs

The symptoms of arthritis vary from day to day. Sometimes a child feels well and moves around quite easily. On other days a joint may flare up – because of an infection, an injury or tiredness, but sometimes for no reason at all. The ups and downs of arthritis can be hard to cope with.

Looking ahead

It is not easy for doctors to say how a person's arthritis will affect them in the future. It usually depends on how long the arthritis has lasted and how much damage has been done to the joints. Children who have only a few inflamed joints usually make a very good recovery. This is less certain for children whose symptoms return, or whose joints are affected more severely each time the illness flares up.

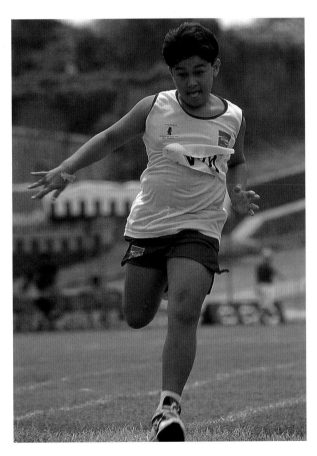

Most children who have arthritis get better as they grow older.

Who has arthritis?

Arthritis can strike at any time, from childhood to old age. It is not an easy condition to adapt to, and each age group faces challenges of its own.

What causes arthritis?

There are many myths about what causes arthritis. The truth is that scientists do not know. There seems to be no single cause, such as climate or diet. Nor is it directly inherited. Doctors suspect that arthritis may be caused by an unusual reaction by the body to an infection.

Juvenile arthritis usually starts in children under the age of five.

Arthritis is *not* caused by:

- Catching cold.
- Getting wet feet.
- Sleeping in a damp bed.
- Eating the wrong foods.
- An injury or fall.

Children with arthritis

Some children develop arthritis when they are very young. This can be a shock to their parents. If a child is too young to understand their condition, the exercises they need to do to treat the arthritis must be gentle and fun.

'Although sometimes it is very painful, arthritis gets easier as I get older because I can understand what is happening around me.'

CLAIRE, AGE 9

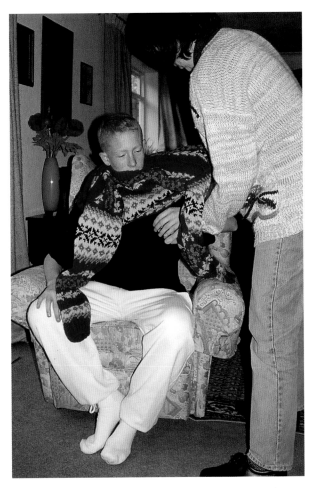

When their joints are sore, a teenager with arthritis may need help to dress.

Teenagers

Some children develop arthritis in their teenage years. The change from being healthy to being ill and even disabled can be difficult. Teenagers like to be independent, but arthritis often limits them. The condition means they have to rely on their parents for help, which may make them feel angry and frustrated.

Older people

Different kinds of arthritis affect older people, too. The condition usually begins between the age of 30 and 50. For many, it brings discomfort, pain and tiredness. Also, a loss of strength and a weaker grip can make hard work of everyday tasks. The effects of arthritis can be hard to cope with, especially for adults who have always been active.

Most types of arthritis affect older people.

Diagnosing arthritis

When children are unwell or in pain, they need to go to the doctor's. Here, they may have some tests that help the doctor to identify the condition – in other words, to make a **diagnosis**.

A tricky diagnosis

It can be difficult to diagnose arthritis in very young children. A two-year-old may not complain about a particular joint, but just be generally grizzly and unhappy. Also, swollen joints are much harder to spot on the plump limbs of a toddler. The first signs of arthritis may be when a child limps, tries to avoid walking, or only uses one hand when playing.

Arthritis is difficult to diagnose in very young children, as they cannot describe what they are feeling.

Is it arthritis?

A child who is limping or complaining of pain in a joint is sent to a **clinic** at a hospital. Here they see a **paediatrician** – a doctor who is an expert in treating children.

The doctor examines the child and asks all sorts of questions. The child has a number of tests, and x-rays may be taken of the affected joints.

Blood tests show up inflammation and anaemia, two important symptoms of arthritis.

If it's not arthritis...

Aches and pains in the body's joints can also be caused by:

- Exercise.
- Stress.
- Cold weather.
- Illnesses, such as German measles or chickenpox.
- An infection of the bone.

After the diagnosis

Making a diagnosis is a slow process, and may take several months. This can be a difficult and worrying time. Eventually, after other possible illnesses have been ruled out, a child may be diagnosed with arthritis. The news often comes as a shock because most people believe the myth that arthritis only affects older people. As they adjust to the diagnosis, both child and parents will have many questions and concerns about the future.

A child who may have arthritis visits the doctor with a parent. It can take many months to diagnose the condition.

13

Treating arthritis

People who have arthritis are treated in several ways. The treatments help to reduce pain and stiffness, slow down the disease and prevent long-term damage to the joints.

A three-in-one treatment
Doctors use three different treatments to combat arthritis:

- drugs, which calm inflammation;
- **physiotherapy**, which helps to keep joints moving;
- **occupational therapy**, which helps people with arthritis to tackle everyday tasks.

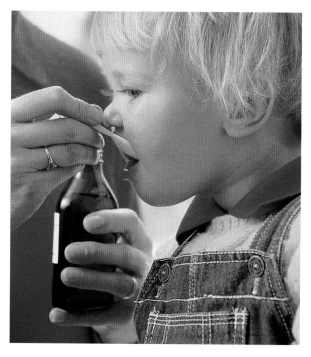

Children with arthritis take medicine every day to ease their swollen joints.

Drugs

Anti-inflammatory drugs reduce inflammation and relieve pain and stiffness in joints. This allows people with arthritis to use their joints as normally as possible and to exercise more easily. More powerful drugs, called **steroids**, are injected into the joints of people whose arthritis has not improved and whose joints are at risk of long-term damage.

Physiotherapy helps to keep joints moving.

A splint gives support to a weak joint, and helps to lessen pain.

Physiotherapy

Physiotherapy uses exercise to fight the effects of arthritis. People who have inflamed joints often hold them in a bent position. This feels more comfortable, but the joints can become very stiff if they are not straightened or exercised regularly. Physiotherapists work out a programme of exercises to keep joints moving as easily as possible, and to strengthen the muscles around them (for more on this, see page 16).

A joint that is badly damaged by arthritis can be replaced. This x-ray shows an artificial hip joint.

Occupational therapy

Occupational therapists advise people with arthritis about tools and equipment to make life easier. They also make **splints** which keep joints in a good position. There are two types of splint – working splints support weak joints, allowing them to be used; resting splints keep joints in the best position while they are not being used. Splints help to relieve pain, reduce swelling and prevent damage to joints.

Surgery

Occasionally, a joint becomes so badly affected by arthritis that an operation is needed to replace it. This is a big operation, but it can greatly improve a person's life.

Who can help?

People with arthritis are cared for by a large medical team. Each member of the team is an expert in their field, and provides a particular kind of care.

Physiotherapists

Physiotherapists plan a programme of exercise, **hydrotherapy** (see page 18) and relaxation to suit the needs of each person with arthritis.

Arthritis often affects the feet. Wearing trainers makes walking more comfortable.

The physiotherapy programme helps to keep an affected joint in a good position, allows the joint to move more easily and strengthens the muscles around it. Physiotherapists suggest treatments to reduce pain, such as placing a hot-water bottle or an ice pack on a sore joint. They may also advise teachers about PE activities for children with arthritis.

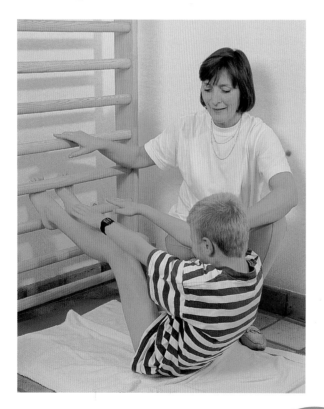

In a physiotherapy session, exercise helps to strengthen muscles, which in turn protects the joints.

Occupational therapists

Occupational therapists visit homes and schools to see how a child carries out everyday tasks, such as bathing, playing, writing or using the stairs. They suggest tools to make life easier, such as a padded pen at school or large-handled knives and forks at home (for more on this see page 23). Occupational therapists make and fit splints too, and advise people on looking after their joints.

Some children with arthritis have as many as four eye tests a year.

Podiatrists

Podiatrists are experts on feet. There are about 35 joints in each foot. Any of these may be affected by arthritis, which can make walking difficult. Podiatrists make special **insoles** to solve this. Insoles hold the feet in a better position.

Ophthalmologists

Ophthalmologists test people's eyes for signs of disease. Children with arthritis may develop a particular type of inflammation in the eye. Regular eye tests help to detect the condition so that it can be treated before the eye is damaged.

Fieldworkers

Fieldworkers are specially trained to help children and their families deal with arthritis. They help solve day-to-day problems, contact schools, and put families in touch so that they can give each other encouragement and support.

A podiatrist is an expert in treating feet.

Exercise for arthritis

Exercise is important for people with arthritis. It keeps joints working, strengthens muscles and helps to reduce pain. But it takes a lot of time and is very hard work.

Making it fun

A person with arthritis needs to exercise one or two times a day. At times, the sessions can be boring and painful. Having to do them makes children with arthritis feel different from their friends. Parents need to be positive and encouraging.

People with arthritis find it easier to exercise in a warm hydrotherapy pool.

It helps to do the exercises at the same time every day, perhaps before a favourite TV programme. Pop music helps with the rhythm of an exercise, and makes the session more fun.

Hydrotherapy

This is a way of exercising in warm water. The water supports the body, and allows someone with arthritis to move more easily without putting weight on their joints.

Exercising to music can be more fun for a child with arthritis.

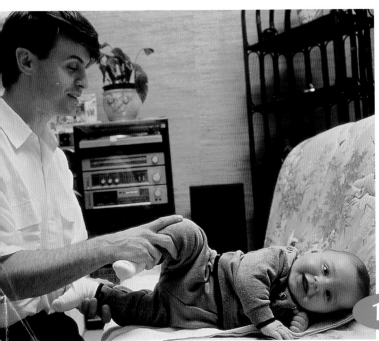

18

Exercising in a hydrotherapy pool helps to strengthen muscles, while the warmth of the water relaxes the muscles and makes joints less painful. The pools are only available in hospitals and special schools, so they can be difficult to find in some parts of the country. But hydrotherapy is fun and useful, and encourages swimming, which is a great form of exercise for children with arthritis.

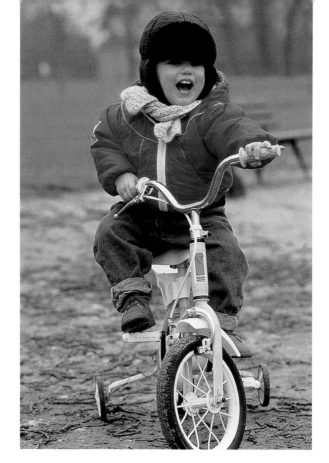

Riding a bicycle exercises the joints in the legs.

Swimming is a good way of exercising without putting a strain on the joints.

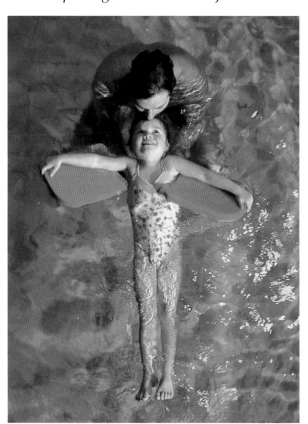

Other activities

Other kinds of exercise can help children with arthritis. The best kinds, such as cycling and walking, help to keep joints moving without straining them. Teenagers with arthritis can go on specially-run weekend breaks where they try out new sports (see page 27).

'Some places have the equipment I need and I even went sailing with my teacher. Once I did a sponsored walk on a special flat route.'
LEANNE, AGE 13

Visiting the clinic

Children with arthritis regularly visit a hospital **clinic**. Here, they may have lots of tests and are examined by members of the medical team.

First visits

When children are first diagnosed with arthritis, they visit their clinic every six weeks or so. Because they have so many people to see, appointments can take hours. Later, when treatment is under way, children visit the clinic less often – about every three to six months.

What happens at the clinic?

Firstly, children are weighed and measured to give an overall picture of how well they are. The doctor asks how they have been since the last visit, whether they are stiff in the morning or have any pain in their joints, and how the arthritis is affecting their everyday life.

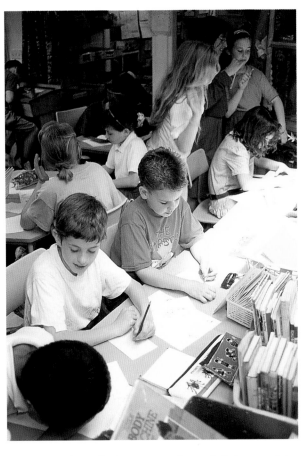

Visits to the clinic mean that children with arthritis miss a lot of school. It can be hard for them to catch up on their work.

Then the doctor looks for any inflammation and checks movement in the affected joints. Comparing the results with those taken at the last visit shows if the condition is improving or not.

Testing, testing

Doctors often ask for x-rays or blood tests to check the progress of the disease. X-rays help them to see whether there has been any damage to the bones. Blood tests show up anaemia and inflammation, and allow doctors to see how the drugs are working. This helps them to decide whether the amount of medicine a child is taking needs to be changed or not.

Children are weighed when they arrive at the clinic.

More appointments

After seeing the doctor, a child with arthritis has appointments with other members of the medical team. The occupational therapist may want to fit a new splint. The podiatrist may need to check a new pair of shoes. The ophthalmologist may need to test the eyes, and perhaps **prescribe** some drops.

'About a year ago we counted that Claire had visited hospital 81 times – we gave up counting after that.'

Mrs Hill

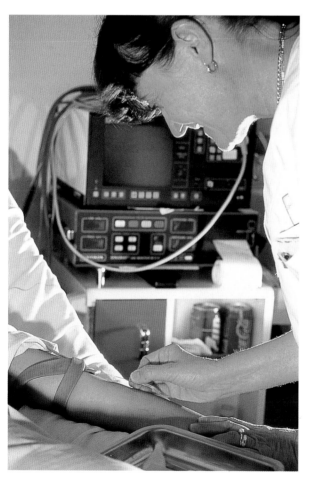

A nurse taking blood for a blood test.

Family life

Arthritis has a big impact on family life. Caring for a young person with arthritis takes a lot of time and energy. It's not surprising that brothers and sisters can feel a little left out.

Finding the time

For someone with arthritis, the day often starts early in the morning with a hot bath to relieve pain and stiffness in the joints.

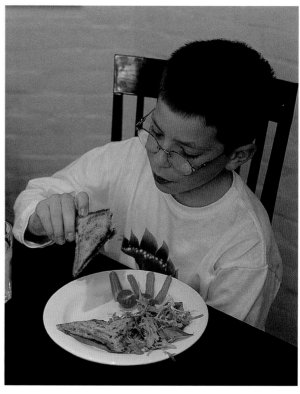

A healthy diet helps to strengthen bones and muscles.

A hot bath in the morning helps to relieve stiff joints.

Simple tasks, such as dressing, take much longer than usual. Time has to be found for hospital visits, exercise and hydrotherapy sessions, too. On top of this, parents spend a lot of time and energy encouraging a child with arthritis to take their medicines, wear their splints and exercise every day.

Diet

People with arthritis do not need to eat a special diet. But they should eat a healthy mixed diet containing **protein** to build up their muscles and **calcium** to strengthen their bones.

Brothers and sisters

Arthritis can affect the other children in a family. Because the disease is so unpredictable, it can cause a lot of last-minute problems. A day out may be cancelled if the child feels unwell. This can be disappointing. Brothers and sisters are usually supportive, but at times they may feel jealous of all the care that a child with arthritis receives.

When a child has arthritis, it affects the whole family.

Special tools, such as this jar opener, make everyday tasks easier.

Changes at home

Occupational therapists often suggest changes to a house to make life easier for people with arthritis – putting in grab rails by a door step and next to the bath and toilet, for example. Special tools and equipment help children perform everyday tasks and become more independent.

Helpful equipment

- Cutlery with bigger handles.
- Padded pens.
- Tap turners.
- Tin and jar openers.
- A stool to perch on.
- An electric toothbrush.

23

Arthritis at school

The hustle and bustle of school life demands many physical skills, and can be a struggle for children with arthritis.

A helping hand

Schools can help a child with arthritis in many ways. The first step is for the parents, teachers, physiotherapist and occupational therapist to discuss the child's needs. The occupational therapist looks for likely problems, such as writing and using stairs. Ramps, padded pens or a computer may be the solution. The child's timetable should be planned to avoid long journeys between lessons.

A busy school staircase may cause problems for a pupil with arthritis.

Sometimes a child needs extra help for a few hours every week. A classroom assistant works next to them, helping them to do physical tasks, such as using scissors, and to keep up with their work.

Writing with the help of a computer may be easier than writing with a pen.

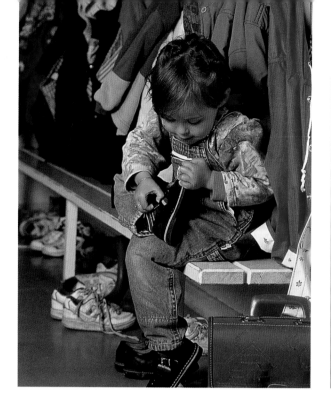

Children with arthritis need more time to get changed than other children.

Schools need to:

- Let children with arthritis play inside with a friend at break.
- Provide them with a lunchtime helper.
- Give them hooks and lockers on the end of a row.
- Allow them to wear trainers.
- Allow them to leave class early to avoid the rush and to give them more time to get around.

Exercise

A physiotherapist can advise schools on exercise. Swimming is very good for children with arthritis. Other sports, such as football or gym, are ruled out because they risk making the inflammation of a joint worse.

Missed lessons

Some children with arthritis miss a lot of school. As well as visiting the clinic, they may need to stay in hospital now and again, for injections or check-ups. Children who miss school can feel left out and it helps if classmates keep in touch. But most children who have arthritis enjoy school life and do well in their work.

Educating others

School staff need to be sensitive to the feelings of children with arthritis. No child wants to stand out from the crowd. Teaching other pupils about arthritis helps a great deal, too. Ignorance about the condition can lead to teasing and even bullying.

Swimming is good for children with arthritis. They can compete equally with others.

Living with arthritis

Living with arthritis is not easy. The condition can prevent people from being independent and doing things that others enjoy. It's important that they have plenty of support.

Being independent

All children learn to become independent; it's an important part of growing up. Most young children can wash and dress themselves from the age of about five, but for a child with serious arthritis this may not be possible before they are ten – perhaps because their joints are just too stiff.

Now and then a person with arthritis may need to walk with crutches, but this is rare.

Learning to dress yourself is an important step on the way to independence.

Young people with arthritis need to practise everyday tasks, such as doing up buttons, turning door handles, going to the toilet and managing stairs. Parents need to avoid being overprotective and should help their children to help themselves, even though this may take a lot of extra time.

Negative attitudes

Many young people find it hard to tell other people that they have arthritis because of the myth that it only affects older people. A few are bullied and teased by children who don't understand what arthritis is.

Being positive

Young people who are picked on for having arthritis may feel that life has handed them a raw deal. They may have low expectations of what they can achieve. But those who are given support enjoy a more positive attitude.

A special break

A normal home and school life is important for children with arthritis, but a weekend away with others who have the same condition can be a real boost. These weekends are specially run for teenagers with arthritis. They provide a break from home, help children to make new friends and give them a taste of activities they may not have tried before. The trips help people to become more confident and realize that they're not alone.

Children with arthritis can try out activities such as canoeing on a weekend break.

Questions people ask

My joints are very sore.
Will exercise damage them?
Exercises do not cause damage.
A physiotherapist can advise on
the best exercises to do and how
often to do them. In the long run,
exercise reduces pain, inflammation
and stiffness, and helps joints to
move more easily. It also makes
muscles stronger. Swimming is
one of the best exercises, and
some pools have sessions when
the water is specially heated.

Joints in the hand are often affected by arthritis. It's important to exercise them.

A lap-top computer can help a child who has problems holding a pen.

**My hands are so stiff that
I find it hard to keep up
at school. What can I do?**
Writing is a problem for many
people with arthritis. Some teachers
give out photocopied notes so that
a child with arthritis doesn't have
to make notes of their own. Padded
or chunky pens can help; so can a
lap-top computer for children who
know how to type. This cuts down
on writing and can make a huge
difference to a child's schoolwork.

Do warmer climates help arthritis?
People all over the world have
arthritis. A warm climate does not
affect the disease itself or prevent
it progressing, but the weather can
affect some people's symptoms.
Some find that warm weather is
better than cold. But for others,
cold crisp days are the best of all.

Will I be able to drive with arthritis?
Most adults with arthritis are able to
drive, but it depends on how severe
their arthritis is. Cars with adjustable
seats and power steering are best.
An automatic car helps, because the
driver does not have to change gear.

*Warm, sunny weather is good for some
people with arthritis. It helps to reduce
swelling and stiffness in their joints.*

Are splints really necessary?
Yes. The aim of a splint is to
make sure a joint stays in the
right position so that when the
arthritis burns itself out – as it
may do – there is little damage
to the bones. When a joint is
uncomfortable, children often
try too hard to protect it and
stop it from moving as it should.
Splints help to correct this.

Glossary

anaemia A condition where there are not enough red cells in the blood. Someone with anaemia feels tired and weak, and looks pale.

anti-inflammatory Designed to reduce swelling and redness in a part of the body.

calcium A chalky white material that is found in bones and which helps to make them hard. Foods such as milk, cheese and yoghurt contain a lot of calcium.

cartilage The smooth, slightly soft and springy material that cushions most of our joints. Cartilage also forms the bendy parts of our skeletons, such as the ridge of the nose.

clinic A place where doctors and nurses treat a particular disease or condition.

diagnosis Discovering what type of disease a person has.

hydrotherapy A type of exercise in warm water that helps stiff joints to move more easily and strengthens muscles.

inflamed Sore, red and swollen.

insole A special lining inside a shoe or boot, sometimes made with extra support or cushioning.

joint A place in the body where two bones meet.

juvenile chronic arthritis A general name for the types of arthritis that affect young people. The word chronic describes something that lasts for a long time.

occupational therapy A type of treatment that helps people to solve problems caused by a condition such as arthritis, and to lead a normal life.

oligo-articular arthritis A type of juvenile arthritis that affects less than five joints.

ophthalmologist An eye expert.

paediatrician A doctor who is an expert in treating children.

physiotherapy A type of treatment that uses exercise to treat someone who has had an accident, an illness or an operation.

podiatrist An expert in treating the feet.

poly-articular arthritis A type of juvenile arthritis that affects five or more joints.

prescribe To recommend a certain drug, medicine or exercise to a patient.

protein A nutrient that the body needs to build new cells and repair itself. Meat, fish and milk contain lots of protein.

splint A device that helps to support a weak or painful joint.

steroids Drugs used to reduce severe inflammation.

symptom One of the signs of a disease. Stiff, inflamed joints are two of the symptoms of arthritis.

synovial fluid The oily liquid that coats a joint and allows the bones to move smoothly and easily.

systemic onset arthritis A type of juvenile arthritis where the child has a high temperature and sometimes a rash, and feels generally unwell.

tissue A group of cells that work together to do a particular job in the body. Muscles and organs are made up of tissue.

vulnerable Open to attack.

x-ray A special photograph that shows up the hard substances inside your body, such as bones and teeth.

Useful organizations

Here are some organizations you can contact for more information about arthritis.

Arthritis Care
18 Stephenson Way
London NW1 2HD

Tel: 020 7916 1500
Website: www.arthritiscare.org.uk

Arthritis Research Campaign (ARC)
St Mary's Court
St Mary's Gate
Chesterfield S41 7DT

Tel: 01246 558033
Website: www.arc.org.uk

Children's Chronic Arthritis
    Association (CCAA)
47 Battenhall Avenue
Worcester WR5 2HN

Tel: 01905 763556

Lady Hoare Trust
First floor, 89 Albert Embankment
London SE1 7TP

Tel: 020 7820 9989
Website: www.ladyhoaretrust.org.uk

Index